OTHER BOOKS BY ANNA RABINOWITZ

At the Site of Inside Out

Darkling: A Poem

The Wanton Sublime: A Florilegium of Whethers and Wonders

PRESENT TENSE

PRESENT TENSE

Anna Rabinowitz

[signature: Anna Rab...]

9/30/10

For Janet + for poetry!

[signature: Anna]

OMNIDAWN PUBLISHING
2010

Cover images courtesy of the Hubble Telescope

Book cover design by Chip Kidd

Book interior design by Ken Keegan

Offset printed in the United States on archival, acid-free recycled paper
by Thomson-Shore, Inc., Dexter, Michigan

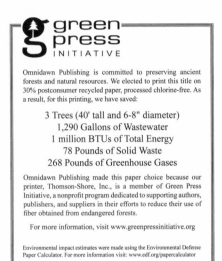

Omnidawn Publishing is committed to preserving ancient
forests and natural resources. We elected to print this title on
30% postconsumer recycled paper, processed chlorine-free. As
a result, for this printing, we have saved:

3 Trees (40' tall and 6-8" diameter)
1,290 Gallons of Wastewater
1 million BTUs of Total Energy
78 Pounds of Solid Waste
268 Pounds of Greenhouse Gases

Omnidawn Publishing made this paper choice because our
printer, Thomson-Shore, Inc., is a member of Green Press
Initiative, a nonprofit program dedicated to supporting authors,
publishers, and suppliers in their efforts to reduce their use of
fiber obtained from endangered forests.

For more information, visit www.greenpressinitiative.org

Environmental impact estimates were made using the Environmental Defense
Paper Calculator. For more information visit: www.edf.org/papercalculator

Library of Congress Catalog-in-Publication Data

Rabinowitz, Anna, 1933-
        Present tense / Anna Rabinowitz.
            p. cm.
        ISBN 978-1-890650-45-2 (pbk. : alk. paper)
        I. Title.
        PS3568.A238P74 2010
        811'.54--dc22

                                        2010020628

Published by Omnidawn Publishing, Richmond, California
                    www.omnidawn.com

        (510) 237-5472   (800) 792-4957

        10 9 8 7 6 5 4 3 2 1

            ISBN: 978-1-890650-45-2

HAPPENINGS

For Marty, Steven, Susan, Nancy, Joel, Alan,
Ethan, Avery, Rachel, and Owen

and then and then and then…

Happening Upon Happening
Among Other Things Happening
In No Particular Order

PROLOGUE

This writing is for the ones who inhabit elsewhere and for those faces that appear on my inner lids as they close, for me with Richie on the tricycle navigating fenced shrubs and cement pathways between blades of grass, for Mr. Bernstein's laundry store redolent of boiled starch, for umbrellas on the beach, waves whacking and wildering, for lying perfectly still while heat runnels through groins, underarms, neck, for the children, good morning, freshing, sparkly day, give me a hug, for my mother who could not stay, for my father who didn't want to, for those denied choice, for hate that stains the playing fields of men, for the appetite of birds after slaughter, the dispersed feathers, for the wild pony in permanent rebellion, for the infant with a blue cheek, for the trees, shoulder to shoulder branching the vastness, wandering the piled shardedness, the intersilvered skies, is information that is gossip and rumor and image, the lies that do not speak their names, is for the loneliness of love that defiles its name, is for others reviled and cast aside, is for the past orphaned, for endurance despite questions forever unanswered, pain that finds no rest, death in a crib, and loss, the hegemony of loss, the shortfalls of memory, how we blunder and plunder, for misadventure, is for duration dressed as eternity which is neither now nor later, nor ever, for cruelty intended and not, is for body parts excised, for body parts replaced, for denial as survival, for the loved ones who exact a price but are themselves rewards and clasp my hand, is for being and erasure, for novelty, experiment, persistent hints of might have been, traces of having been, come back momentary sisters, is for how we are, how it is, come back fragmentary brothers, where we were we are here and where we are and not to be and where there is a there not yet and still to be

ACT I

The Anatomy of Present Tense

A HISTORY OF TIME I

Time bolts from the scheme
Into our meager
Mouths—weeks, hours
Fist to a clot—
Pellets of time

Pound precincts of dream.
In new-grown gear
Bones uncower,
Buck from the grave plot
Into time that this time

Speeds back. We dream
What was will be; we age younger,
Each moment empower
What has come to go: white
Hair browns, withered skin unlines,

Grayed eyes blue. But, if in time
Leaves tree and stems defer
To root, if buds deflower
And earth broods dark with light,
What stokes the ash to flame again?

PRESENT TENSE I

Nostalgia is a Loaded Gun

We've traded the hiss, the fuzz and the fizz of the fair for elsewhere, a landmark in the riddled dark of "why is a raven like a writing desk?"

We laugh when we can no longer cry and last laughs brood longest.

Sunrise entreats us with Goya disasters of war, Munch forests, and Warhol electric chairs.

Pre-emptive fictions and futile plots unmask reality as a triumph of open wounds.

David Lynch once said, "images are no longer beautiful, but chains are."

Oil fields and T-shirts are now extinct.

Fourteen-foot fences fail to enclose dissolute goals and murderous needs.

As for abstract marks or loving gestures, those strokes no longer seize the eye.

To fabricate is to make and to fake.

Lies are the intensest truths.

Oh, how we miss fertilized hair and lacquered toenail clippings shaped into red-ripe cherries.

Who can take pride in bottling the sweat of beleaguered brows for sale to the highest bidder?

If only we could costume memories. But our headmasters refuse to learn from old clothes.

If only we could find radiance in the forlorn.

I have always been a dreamer.

So tell us what we're fighting for

We want to know, deathless commander

           Sound off onetwo

     From you
        all the worlds

          From you
             something from nothing

Sound off threefour

    contraction

        concealment

    huptwothreefour

A great inhale

    of you

       to you

A grenade within you

From the center

Therefore the story has no center

OOOOOOO   *huptwothreefour*

The circumference too

Withdrawal as a violence of void

sparks as your fracture of lights

Vessels shattered
so tell us what we're fighting for

WE   the dying ones

messengers
workhorses
tools

leftright leftright leftright

left

to placate the shards

A HISTORY OF TIME II

Time—
           sped, lost, gone

When we are dead we are late

Perpetually late

           once we're late

Clock, calendar halt

The work wrestles with time

     It will be late
When claimed by time
               or right on time

Lateness arrives for unmaking
For the sprawl and the drip
The view of the abyss
Over which the bridge now sways

For being everywhere in the nowhere

For the all-at-once

The unreconciled that is impossible
The exiled that is truth

The impertinence now pertinent

PRIMER

1.

Extrude light from darkness.
When day breaks scoop up shards.

Ask time to make the pieces fit.
Who has more leisure than time?

> *Eternity is a very long time, especially*
> *towards the end.*

2.

Slice into a section of the waters.
Place heaven between the margins,
Give it a long arm and an index finger
pointed in your direction. Ask
if you are being scolded
or invited to proceed.

> *The struggle itself toward the*
> *heights is enough to fill a man's heart.*

3.

Sow seeds for grass, herbs, trees, and greed.

> *It is not your obligation to complete the task, but neither are you at*
> *liberty to desist from it entirely…*

4.

Invent signs and portents:
Monsters of the deep, for example.
Financial frauds,
Weapons of mass destruction.
Slip them into your pocket.

They're bound to come in handy one day.

> *E cosi desiro me mena*—and so desire
> carries me along.

5.

Tat a poem with lacework that swims.
Compose an essay with heaving geometries of air and sea.
Encase three perfect flowers in an elegant vitrine.

Invention is the mother of intention.

> *All warfare is based on deception.*

6.

Subdue dust dervishing around you.
Gaze in the mirror as you shape
A few handfuls between moistened palms.

Model carefully with an additive of clay.
You will produce all the companions you'll ever need.

When it is dark beware of your new friends.

> *The soul is here for its own joy.*

7.

Talk to stone. Tell it words
you want it to remember.

Have stone repeat these words
three times after you.

Do this one hundred times a day
for the rest of your life.

On the last day go to stone
and ask it what it knows.

> *For we are but of yesterday, and know nothing,*
> *Because our days upon earth are a shadow—*

CHIEF SEATTLE SPEAKS

You folks observe the changers
Who have come to this land

And our progeny will
Watch and learn from them now
And those who will come after us
Our children

And they will become just like
The same
As the changers who have come to us
On this land
You folks observe them well

Your religion
Was written on tablets of stone
By the iron finger of an angry God
Lest you forget

The red man could never comprehend
Nor remember it

Our religion
Is the tradition of our ancestors
The dreams of our old men
Given to them
In the solemn hours of the night
By the great spirit
And the visions of our leaders
And it is written in the hearts of our people

Your dead cease to love you
And leave the land of their nativity
As soon as they pass the portals of the tomb

They wander far away
Beyond the stars
And are soon forgotten and never return

Our dead never forget
This beautiful world that gave them being

They always love
Its winding rivers
Its sacred mountains
And its sequestered vales…

And they ever yearn in tenderest affection over
The lonely-hearted living
And often return to visit, guide and comfort them

We will ponder your proposition and when we decide we will tell you

There is no death
Only a change of worlds

PRESENT TENSE II

Our Lives are Crowded Battered Woods

Dawns are terribly groggy.

Nights are relentlessly cold.

They took us away; they bound us with ropes; they put us in boats. They could not say they were proud or happy. We were the ones who taught them historic decision.

We all know facts keep trying to escape the harsh logic of the homeland.

Still, there are some who continue to believe in self-improvement. They study etiquette and refine new culinary skills.

Others reminisce about art auction bids and weapons they packed when invited to weekend hunts.

"Leash Girl" still refuses to ponder barbaric glee.

Playgrounds are sown with guns, knives, and sorrowing seed.

Reality is a bottomless mouth.

I have felt alien every day of my life.

Oh gods have you forsaken us now and for all?

A gust of blood puddles the rug;
roses dash in the other direction
where endearments are uppermost
but the true path ineluctably muddied.

Even the voyeur who is not a spy
barely sees what's in front of his nose
though he peers hard with his ear and his hands.

Only one more shot remains on the roll.

Multiple charges pulse
with a gluttony sparked by starry skies
and the trenchant moon in its rigged figments.

We do not want our appetites made sport
or lapped up by wanton
winds' digressions with rain.

We do not want our desires daunted that way.

We had hoped they would slip their tongues
into our mouths and cruise our plights,
quicksilver lusts hot to shimmy all night,

not these come-lately words
hunted down by combatants lying in wait
for the ideal moment to pull out their guns.

GUN MOOSE SNOW

Patience. Dawn. Her long wait's not been a waste.
His shoulders come within range of her site.

One bullet between his eyes will seal
                              an end to roaming free.

"Pay dirt! I've hit pay dirt," she squeals with glee.

So it goes:
                blood-letting—
                              unraveled chevrons of crimson
                                        darn white snow, a toppled body
            ringed by the broad, black wheel
Of eagleflight.

His amber pile,
            riddled by hoarfrost,
Punctures the lowering dark
                with stippled light.

Rivers clotted with ice lumber through frozen fields.

PRESENT TENSE III

Outskirts of the Fractured Glow

Survival, denial, resistance, escape are monkeys riding our backs.

We try to find the sublime but nightmares ambush our quest.

It's now or never. We must quicken our evasions with slogan and jest.

We must relish time's booty of arcana smoking at the altars of our worship of youth.

Even the defunct deserves a place in the commotion of the soul.

What is more tender, more intimate than tree houses made of old socks nestled in bare branches?

I had hoped sun salutes would prolong my use...

INTERVIEW 1992

Interviewer: *Why do you kill children?*

Serbian Soldier: *Because someday they will grow up and we will have to kill them then.*

PRESENT TENSE IV

We Had Stalked the Doe

Commerce. Production. Consumption. Who makes? Who takes?

It's useless to give up cashmere shawls, gold armatures, SUVs, furs and silks to achieve cross-cultural pollination or transcendence.

Since we've ceased to celebrate works-in-progress or cutting-edge sound bites, we photograph commodities to provide a permanent record of desire in the grass and under the elms.

Turkey on the chairlift.

Rooster in the coop.

Testimony is a cryptic relic deformed by the violence of authority.

We recall the limited palette of ashen tones when we drove through Eastern Europe. Billboards, even in Estonia, summoned up fascinations with dieting, alcoholism and psychotherapy.

Should we have eaten those salads of language?

Should we have risked teased hairstyles and gained weight?

Should we have giggled amidst severest woe?

Mimicry, idolatry, fanaticism, greed. Oh, fervid, tangled brushwork, what can we do to hold you at bay?

I am old. I am old. The good day grows cold.

Suppose we rut trenches
    with carcasses of children,

        tuck corpses into body bags

tufted with carnage for fill.

Suppose we fall to our knees

    in the name of freedom;

        suppose we braid slogans
            to scarf round our throats.

Suppose we mass sandcastles
      against onslaughts of ash,
battalions of wound.

      Suppose
trenches impastoed with bone.

Suppose we blast and we batter,

    inject bombs with the serum
      of right-minded, remedial urge,

bodies exploding like rockets in air.

Suppose ejaculations of flame
hosannahed from oil-glutted fields,

legions of eyegouge and molten ear

graffitied on rockslide and mud.

Suppose skulls leering jawfuls of uniform
white teeth, limbs restitched to marching hearts,

Old Glory infected with catchword and lie,

and mothers, in the ditches of overstuffed sofas,

strand by strand unplugging their scalps.

PRESENT TENSE V

The Power to Kill's a Wandering Cloud

Daily we labor to compile lists of cars used as bombs in the late Middle East.

Some claim the death knell sounded when we failed to interface with nature.

Surely, daisies heard the bugles' sound. Even if that's true, what could daisies have done?

Tectonic plates move at the same rate our fingernails grow. Does this prove we're connected to the cosmos after all?

The time's deranged. Music is pathologically cheerful. Melancholy, mutilation, molestation dominate the national unconsciousness.

We cuddle with lascivious tigers, jailbait blondes, sound bites, and mutable lies.

To say nothing of the chutzpah of poodles crashing pit bull parties.

The center will not hold. Nor the peripheries…that are nowhere. This has nothing to do with childhood wonder or encounters in restroom stalls.

Everything's on the verge of falling or floating away.

We've been told to delight in the illicit, the light cast on succulent, silicone-plumped breasts, the vaginal gravitas of slits in the wall, the ribald humor of hot dogs slathered with mustard and dipped in crème fraiche.

Still, nothing is more tender, more intimate than tree houses made of old socks nestled in bare branches.

I have always been estranged.

Where is the place that love dwelleth?

Je suis dans la chambre de ma mere.

"Fear and sorrow are the true characters and inseparable companions of
most melancholy."

AND VIOLENCE? AND WAR? AND ARROGANCE?

Why do we do this?

Where is the place that love
dwelleth?

Let it commence
Let it amaze
Let it be strangelove, strangeplace, strangewhere
Let it be shaved rock
Let it be lavender lakes
Let it be sunscrawl
Let it be tussock and flocked grass
Let it be revels of green
Let it be fields of faith
Let it be quarrels with fate
Let it ravish and grieve
Let it be leeway and curb
The unguarded eye
Kohlsmudge and drowse
Let it be lust behind veils
Let it be lust unchained
Let it be the invention of forgiving
The intention of amends
Let it not be contention
Let it be finch nests and peacock splay
Cobra stream and branch-branded sky
Let it be pilgrims, nomads
Prodigals gone home
Let it be horses, goats
Fanfares of cow
Showdowns of gull
Let it not be play-possum pose
Let it provoke
Let it vex
Let it be half-easeful with risk
Let it be dismantled walls
Weepdirge and bleat of denuded trees
Barkgnarl, barksnarl
Scruff-brushed grammars of comma and dash
Let it not be grudge
Let it be sandblush

Let it be dogmas in dust
Let it not be eras of rain
Let it not be drought and baked clay
Let it be caravans pelted by *where*
Let it be sorcery and ghost
Let it not be bleached bones
Let it be unraveled birdpeal teasing the trees
Let it be stanzas pursued by vanishing feet
Let it not be islands of hiding and void
Let it not be parlance of shame
Let it be rails flushed from the reeds
Let it be old habits of umbrage forced to their knees
Let it be stalemates of rage
Let it not be wrongs clinging like burrs to the fur of the tongue
Let it be patience
Slackening of rope
Waterwheel slowed
Let it be tender truce
Victims unloosed
Let it unflinch, unbend, unscruple
Let it relent and cease
Let it not be posthumous

ACT II

The Invention of Violence

THE GOOD BOOK

CAIN

And when they were in the field,
Cain rose up against his brother Abel,
and killed him.
(Genesis 4:8)

> twitching, the lilacs
> sprang to bloom

If I am not for myself, who will be for me?
And if I am only for myself, what am I?
And if not now, when?

LAMECH

I have killed a man for wounding me,
a young man for striking me.
(Genesis 4:23)

> outside, light played,
> seeing with blindness

And there was light and it could not be explained,
nor did anyone want that. And then there was wanting
to say but not to be heard, not to be understood
simply to make the sounds, to do the thing.

YAHWEH

Then the Lord rained on Sodom and Gomorrah
sulfur and fire from the Lord out of Heaven;

and he overthrew those cities, and all the Plain,
and all the inhabitants of the cities,
and what grew on the ground.
(Genesis 4:24–25)

and man wrought parsible
concussions, hearing god

JACOB

Simeon and Levi are brothers;
weapons of violence are their swords.

May I not be joined to their company—
for in their anger they killed men,
and at their whim they hamstrung oxen.
Cursed be their anger, for it is fierce,
and their wrath
for it is cruel!
(Genesis 49:5–7)

an urgency honed on
thick-throated swords

And the id sang out.

YAHWEH

If the offering is a burnt offering from the herd,
you shall offer a male without blemish.
(Leviticus 1:3)

god was a ravenous god
a mouth before words

YAHWEH

And the Canaanite King fought against Israel…

Then Israel made a vow to the Lord and said,
'If you will indeed give this people into our hands,
then we will utterly destroy their towns.'
The Lord…handed over the Canaanites;
and they utterly destroyed them and their towns.
(Numbers 21:1–3)

god was a high-grade fever,
a third-degree burn

Year after year
on the monkey's face,
a monkey face.

YAHWEH

Then King Og came out against the Israelites.

So they killed him, his sons, and all his people,
until there was no survivor left;
and they took possession of his land.
(Numbers 21:33–35)

god was brutal waste, the taste
of ash and torrid stone

—that ole devil love

MOSES

...and we utterly destroyed them, as we had done to
King Sihon of Heshbon,
in each city utterly destroying men, women and children.
But all the livestock and plunder of the towns
we kept as spoil for ourselves.
(Deuteronomy 3:6–7)

tender flesh sated god
marbled, marrow-boned

YAHWEH

Your own eyes have seen everything
that the Lord your God has done to these two kings;
so the Lord will do to all the kingdoms
into which you are about to cross.
Do not fear them, for it is the Lord your God who fights for you.
(Deuteronomy 3:21–22)

god inhaled, making room
and war awaited man, before man

They will wait in forests,
on mountains, in caves, in sheds
and animal stalls, crawl spaces,
stables, crates, silently in their tiny
shelters. And when they emerge,
will they be blind, atrophied,
their limbs tangled,
severed, or numb?

MOSES

I will make my arrows drunk with blood,
and my sword shall devour flesh—
(Deuteronomy 3:42)

and man found the means
and it was good

and the libido sang out…

JOSHUA

And Joshua burned down the city of Jericho, and Joshua
stretched out his sword and made the city of Ai
a great heap of stones which stands there to this day.
And when the five Amorite kings camped against
Gibeon and made war against it,
…the Lord threw down huge stones from heaven on them
…and they died…
(Joshua 8:29)

and the sun beamed
and the moon cheered

JOSHUA

And Joshua put his feet on the necks of 31 kings, kings of:

Jericho
Ai
Jerusalem
Jarmuth
Makkedah

                         Libnah
                         Lachish
                          Gezer
                          Eglon
                         Hebron
                          Debir
                          Geder
                         Hormah
                          Arad
                         Adullam
                          Bethel
                         Tappuah
                         Hepher
                          Aphek
                         Lasharon
                          Madon
                          Hazor
                     Shimron-meron
                        Achshaph
                         Taanach
                         Megiddo
                          Kedesh
                    Jokneam in Carmel
                    Dor in Naphath-dor
                     Goiim in Galilee
                          Tirzah

         for the Lord fought for Israel.

                              And the Israelites put
                              away all other gods…

In Bresson's film "Lancelot of the Lake",
After too many dead
And too much blood shed,

Guinevere tells Lancelot he sought
God,
                    not the Grail—

God—elusive, evasive, unseen, unknown,
Off in the elsewhere, somewhere, nowhere—

Carnivore starved for human flesh
(Will he never get his fill?)

Seated on his throne of immolation
Loving us to pieces, as we do our children,
Lusting to eat us up...

It's a matter of creation
                    and possession,

The anguish of desire

ANNA SPEAKS

Perhaps I should let you in
On the time I threw a knife
At my brother.

Neither of us remembers
What made me do it, why him
As the target,

Why me on the offensive
Trying to get something out
Of my system,

Just that I was mad as hell,
The blade gleamed on the table,
And he was there.

Belated kerfuffle in a belated place,
          And the opulent penny hunkers on the sill

While the door slams its back

     To the wind and rain the window abhors.

The opulent penny hunkers on the sill
          Though it covets the bed plumped for love
The wind and rain and window ignore.

The table bursts out with a *do re mi fa*
                    to the moon-struck bed plumped for love.

The sofa of song belts out high C's.

     The table staccatos *do re mi fa,*

The chair yowls, the desk drones
To the sofa of song's butchered high C's,

Fractured discord courts harmonic debris:

          Chair aclack, desk ayelp, stool acraze,

          Clash, jam, jangle, jig the daily serenade:

Blustery discourse of harmonic debris.

          Crescendo/diminuendo: the door comes unhinged,

          Beats time *agitato* as the daily serenade
          Brays its clamor of chords in belated place.

skies hurl griefs   hot and bleak

      sky-dredged griefs

famine, torture bulls-eyed by scorch
                       (and heaven too?)

black holes harangue ash-slogged flame

brutal agendas   (as in tens of thousands slaughtered or sold)
      brace at the cusp

as when bombs beg translation

      corruption
   in the throes (at the close?) of speech

      declining a text

         as when words
shed reason
         as when prayer
dreads sound

         as in
laments smashed on the paved

     whose vowels
        (unkempt off the air)
plead for verbs   trail toxic mouths

WHY DO WE DO THIS

      FOR WHAT REASON

unspeakable dictions smeared on rubbled slate
landscapes defaced by grief
despair drained of (fraught with?) nuance

out and down   down and down

a story is being told

it is simple

I do not understand

it does not hold   it will not hold

it must not hold

Is there a place where love dwelleth?

The new century

    and nine months

        From the sky a great King of Terror
        A great liquidation depletes the sky

The sky ignites

Roils in a great collapse,
        Brothers are ripped apart

GREAT   GREAT

We did not seek great this day, not this

Ordinary day crazed by sunsear

        Not this scourge of weather

A war by any other name would smell as

Rank as Desert Storm steeping in the pot, in spite
Of the fact that we expected a brew less explosive,
Some event less excessive than thousands of futures slipping away, less
Eradicable—a safer ambiance, like Flags Waving at Noon or

Bombs Bursting With Scree, perhaps a surge of
Yankees At Morn to nudge the quotidian from complacency, to

Annihilate all terrorists in the plot, injecting Democracy
Nearer The Front Lines where nouns still wade about, before
Yardsticks pummel our brains with questions about the Measure

Of Naming.—
     First Flush of Passion, Darjeeling Murders
Tonight,
     The time has come to Drive
Home the Zingers.
     Ah, Mayhem Of Bomb! Oh, Medley of Oils! Convoys Of Hate!
     Detonation Of Troops In
Erroneous Zones!

               When will the kettle whistle true?
                  Where, on
Ruin-wracked miles,
     while Chamomile Quietly Smiles, can we

Nail these words—high teas for never again and peace
                      in our time—
As our real intention, not to mention prayer, not to
Mention obsession—even sacrifice—
Eons before these words set out to rustle leaves?

ACT III

Doomsday for Galaxies

ALBERT SIGMUND BITTER FRUIT

1931
Dear Dr. Freud:
...This is the problem. Is there any way of delivering mankind from the menace of war?

Dear Mr. Einstein:
I expected you to choose a problem lying on the borderland of the knowable, as it stands today a theme which each of us, physicist and psychologist, might approach from his own angle, to meet at last on common ground, though setting out from different premises. Thus the question which you put me—what is to be done to rid mankind of the war menace?—took me by surprise.

Dear Dr. Freud:
...the ruling class...has the schools and press, usually the Church as well, under its thumb. This enables it to organize and sway the emotions of the masses, and makes its tool of them... How is it that these devices succeed so well in rousing men to such wild enthusiasm, even to sacrifice their lives? Only one answer is possible. Because man has within him a lust for hatred and destruction.

Dear Mr. Einstein:
I entirely agree with you. I believe in the existence of this instinct... Conflicts of interest between man and man are resolved...by the recourse to violence....

———

1950
Dear Mankind:
I know not with what weapons World War III will be fought but World War IV will be fought with sticks and stones.

———

2009
To Whom It May Concern:

It is between us and the wine-dark sea...

Millennia are held at bay, the credos know their place,
The gravel throat reveals she plays with microphones and lace,
The ice cream cones storm center stage beset by flagrant lights,
And roses skipping from the wings demand their equal rights.

The world's a gas, so diddle dee. Oh nonny no the vapors flow.
The world's a glass. It hosts our rub to rose its rosey glow.

The plot is tall, the humans short, it matters not at all
That count-downs rage, that tongues grow wild, that crass eyes
    come to call.
The acts poseur, the dancers split, their twists unjig the scene;
With mouths stained red they thickly smooch rigged flavors on
    the screen.

The world's a gas, so diddle dee. Oh nonny no, the trumpets crow.
The world's a glass. It begs a scrub to toast its rosey glow.

The evidence that huddles there across the wide divide
Where angels rear and windows peer and bikers hit their stride
Is stuffed with bread and cigarettes, with bitten backs and knees,
As svelte batons tweek-tap sleek beats to fluff the loose-leafed trees.

The world's a gas, so diddle dee. Oh nonny no how do we know?
The world's a glass. It licks its lips to taste for rosey glow.

The flasher comes to flip her skirt, the vixen hurls her hair
While stagehands broom the bloomy stems, and petals rose the air.
Stilletto heels kick up plump toes and fingers flex to nail
The window washer loping left, then pirouetting with his pail.

The world's a gas, so diddle dee. Oh nonny no where do we go?
The world's a glass. It craves the view and cranes for rosey glow.

The aftermath is lowered down, the scaffolding goes up.
The beepers squeak, the sensors squeal, we kids shriek in our cups.
Ten squeegees roam the foggy panes, the washer gropes on tippy toes,
But *Sturm und Drang* upstage the lot midst tweetling dozey does.

The world's a gas, oh diddle dee, and nonny no to seeds we stow.
The world's a glass where humans crash on rosey glow.

All afternoon alterities advance—
    afars abdicate—
        and azure anons abandon the air—

      and

Beyond blue—betrayal, blasphemy, brimstone, and bray—

      blind bards' bereaved ballads beached
          on bygones of bearded beliefs—

COULD WE HAVE CALLED FOR A CESSATION OF CLAMORS—

     COULD WE HAVE CAUTIONED
         CRIMSON NOT TO COLONIZE ITS CURRENCIES
         ON CATAFALQUES OF

DUN—to dodge their devils—those

    deathdrizzling   dreaddroning   dreardoting

       drillmerchants of deal—

Entropy and elans of eclipse—
       emerald and the envy of ecru—

        ETERNITY AND THE ERRORS OF EL—

Fractured fuchsias fueled
    by frontmen flexed for the fray—

      flash-frozen futures

Gone glottal   gone global

O grizzly gunfire
      grassed in gray grammar—

O grim geography

Hounding the hungry horoscope—
      hardworking harbinger—
            our hyacinth of hope—

Inland ideologies infect incunabula
      inferences ignite innuendos
    and invaders inject ivory ire in inks—

January Junes—
    jardins jam—
      jonquils jealous for

Knowledge of khaki and kohl kow-tow
      to karma and ken—

Lavender lets legions—
    lavender leers—
      lavender lures leitmotifs landward to

Mollify maverick mauves—
      the marl and the maelstrom of money and might

    mortgaged mayhem of markets
      masked, mazed and marooned by

Necromancing navy nostalgias of the
    numberless numerous
      numbed by the nonce of night's noon—

ONSLAUGHT OF OCHRE, ONTOGENY OF OBLIVION—

      oracular omens ogle

Postscripts of paid product placement, profit proliferation,
      and puce pandemonium polluting the port—

Quotidians quaqua quite quixotically—
      quests quake and
         quit the quays—

Ruby rides rain—

      READER   IS THIS RHETORIC OR REALISM

        REDDENED AND ROUGED—

STRAPHANGERS

      ARE WE SCARLET OR SEPIA
          SURFSURGE OR SLAM—

      ARE WE SELLER OR SOLD—

Trophy the true—
      tango the traipse—
        tidy the taupe—
            O terrestrial tourists

Un-umber ulterior's unanimous urge—

Very vermilion the virtual void—
      valiant the verge—

Weltschmerz of weathers—
                woundweary whites—

                whither our windows
        our wardrobes   our warbles   our woes

        whilst

Xanadu xanthenes and X xes X—

Yammer yes yammer yes yowlyelp
                you yellowedyearyesteryore yens

                yonder yearn yarrow
                                and yodeling yews
        yonder young
Zinnias zaffer the zeds—

        ZEITGEIST   MY ZEITGEIST   ZUPPA DI ZOOS (ZEUS)

                ZERO, O ZERO, OUR ZEALOTSTREWN ZONES—

REB MEIR SPEAKS

I say the world's a fair: trade a little, sell, bargain, buy a shirt or two,
  Stall to wagon, poultry, eggs, butter, cheese, onions for the fish,
Fingers into action for the final count, coins from corners of kerchiefs.
  Capmakers, coatmakers, shoemakers, bakers, my fellow Jews,

  I say the world's a fair. Does good faith embrace your every trade?
Do you keep thumbs from the scale? Do you knead dough with clean hands?
    Are your arms soft with desire or stiff with demand?
    And, tell me, what you acquire—is it what you need?

In this time

    in isolate rooms

of brow-beaten cities   dirt-sodden villages   grimy
    towns

each puts a hand in a pocket   opens a drawer

       rummages in a purse

    takes out the coin

       and sets it on end

some on the floor   on mirror   on a table

    some on the back of the hand

       tip of the nose

          nail of the large toe

       flat of an arm

in some places some go outdoors to spin their coins

at the curb of the lane   on the sidewalk

on the slate of a garden path

on rooftops
at the foot of mountains

into caves and low valleys

earth barnacled with coin

priceless common denominators

gathering momentum

ceaseless tireless

ONECOINANOTHERCOINANOTHERCOINANOTHER

PLAYMATES SING

Playmate, come out and play with me
And rub your weapons three
Between my spreading knees
Slide through my open door
And we'll be lovers true forever more

It was a storm-wracked day
He couldn't come to play
With blood-shot eyes and wounded sighs
We could hear him say:

Forgive me, Playmate, I cannot play with you
My dick's not here to screw
Boo-hoo, hoo hoo
Can't pet your thumping thighs
So close your open door
I'm hard, it's true, and off to war

TAPED FROM EARLIER LIVE PODCASTS

Left, left, left

Right   left

Bulletin I

On Friday Saturday will
Gust low to strut in the face
Of heavy sunshine.
At the northern heights
Evening will rise and file out.

I left my wife in Pennsylvania
With official lies and a Prez with a grin and a wild-west mania—
Itching to fight, the guy yacked with god and oil lubed his brainia

I thought I was right; I thought he was right
Right for my country and right for the world

AND WHOOP-DEE-DOO

The crime's a damn joke on me and you

Bulletin II

Sunday lays low
To mobilize today.
Boundaries are drawn
To kidnap afternoon.

A showdown in blustery skies
Threatens to seal our doom.

Left, left I left my life in New Orleans
With boy-girl twins and a flood-load of liens
And a Prez with no clue to what bad news means

I thought I was right; I thought he was right
Right for my country and right for the world
I thought it was right, right

AND WHOOP-DEE-DOO

The knock's at the door and
Death's got the hots for me and you

Bulletin III

Forces continue to race along the eastern tier.
The system marches from rear lines
To the raveled brink of the moon.
The isolate will intensify.

Spotlights gain a foothold along the shore,
But the immediate sector
Is dredged by aimless
Ranks of an untrained rebel flank.

Left, left, left right, I left my kids on the streets of starvation
With Fritos and Ring Dings to pass for nutrition
And a Prez with a smirk and a holy mission

Did I do right, right?

Right for my country, the others, or me
Did I do right
To hitch my hide to

WHOOP-DE-DOO

To speak in tongues
And hear askew
The laugh, ha ha's, on me and you

Bulletin IV

Long before defeat slopes
To the sea, departure drizzles the air.
The danger of terror is within range.
Much colder fleeces the certain demise.
The security of weather grinds to a halt.

Remain stationary. Be pacific.
Do not board frighted winds,
Passing buses or armored tanks.
The most hit-or-miss system on record now blows.

Left, left I had a good home and I left
I had a good wife and I left
I enlisted one day and it served me right

Right where the shell mince-meated both knees
And the Prez revs up his grin and lies through his teeth

WHOOP-DE-DOO

Buddy boy god, come down for a spin
And lasso me in for a finger-lickin' win.

Bulletin V

Widespread portions will rally
While late-night maneuvers panhandle
Briskly for beyond-disclaimer stakes.
Stalled tactics fuel a mix
Of weakened defenses competing
With surges of energy unable to strike.

Hot nights and cold days will accelerate
Corridors of stubborn jeopardy.

There are new furies on the moon.

Rest assured, the dead and injured
will be flown home only at night

                                        Left, left, left

                        Right   left
                Right   left

            Don't sit under the apple tree
            With anyone else but me
            With anyone else but me
            No, no, no
            'Til I come marching home.

WILLIAM SIEGFRIED BITTER ASPIC

WB: *The Kings of Asia heard*
The howl rise up from Europe!

Why live in unquenchable burnings?

SS: *The long parades are done.*
The darkness tells how vainly I have striven.

WB: *And their children wept, & built*
Tombs in the desolate places

And they left the pendulous earth.

SS: *Up a disconsolate straggling village street*
I saw the tired troops trudge: I heard their tired feet
…nearer, day by day,

To the foul beast of war…

WB: *Let others study Art:*
Rome has somewhat better to do,
Namely War & Dominion.

Cruelty has a human heart.

SS: *And trunks face downward in the sucking mud,*
And naked, sodden buttocks, mats of hair,
Bulged, clotted heads sleep in the plastering slime,

And then the rain begins—the jolly old rain!

"I saw the survivors of a battle sending out postcards."

And the card said:

WRITE NOTHING ON THIS SIDE
EXCEPT THE DATE AND YOUR SIGNATURE

Select the correct answer.

I am quite well.

You will be pleased to know I have been cited for
- ❏ A tenacious urge to battle extremes of rodents.
- ❏ A brash indifference to personal safety.
- ❏ Intrepid skill when eating sand.
- ❏ Failure to file my tax return.

Since I have
- ❏ lost my left leg, both hands, and the song in my heart
- ❏ not lost my left leg, both hands, and the song in my heart

I ❏ abhor consolation.
- ❏ demand consolation.

Please greet me with ❏ uproarious jokes.
- ❏ a cherry coke.
- ❏ an American flag pin.

Meet me at <u>FOREVERMORE at the intersection of Loss and Memory</u>

Signature only _____

Date _____

The one who hardens the heart
        slithers into evil

through whose veins seeps venom
burrows through smoke

          comrade of worms   eroder of stone

exiled to silence
        as verdict against speech

    consigned to shadows

          wherein shallows…

              wherein doom…

Hearts smolder in mute reaches
Hearts blacken in unblossoming

(and still)

    we sit and eat and tend our tongues

        Whereof one cannot speak

        thereof be silent

        Whereof one must speak

        thereof be heard

Unfurled
offering in the unsay

In silence do not pass

bypass   pass over

pass by

When the temple burned silence prowled

when ovens raged

silence ground its teeth

on corpsestrewn pyres

The high sky slides down

infalling   indwelling

OUT AND DOWN   HERE AND NOW

nomore nomore with ribbons on the town

Had they been given the choice:

throatloads of choked voice

locked in knots of smothered

othered utterance

Had we unbound our swaddled tongues...

Had earth ceased circling when they plunged
into thunderous dispersal...

wherein silence was rank...

whereby silence sank...

NOTES: COERCIVE COUNTERINTELLIGENCE INTERROGATION OF RESISTANT SOURCES

HOW TO SUCCEED IN TORTURE
WITHOUT REALLY TRYING

1. FIRST THINGS FIRST:

Surprise,
        catch your source off balance
        when he least expects it:
At the moment he opens his eyes in the morning
While he shits on the can.

Detain and confine,

            quickly,
                        quickly

        cut him off from the known.

Plunge your source into the strange,

            the invisible wells gone dry in his bones
Drained by his eyes

        He's in occupied territory—

        he could walk a long time and find nowhere, nothing, nada

        no doors, no tunnels, windows

2. KEEP IT SIMPLE:

Familiar clothing reinforces identity.

Replace the source's attire with items several sizes too large.

Shave off his hair.

Confiscate his belt; make him hold up his pants.

Best of all, keep him naked, especially from the waist down.

3. YOUR GOALS:

Identify, expose and exploit the resistant source's internal hungers.

Induce the source to fluctuate inside himself.

Befuddle the source's anxiety with constant, sudden disruptions of patterns, blurs and howling winds.

Make sure the source's body is havoc and there is no escape.

Play the role of superior external/paternal power geared to crush the source's will and extract a true confession.

NOTA BENE: the interrogator, by virtue of his role as the sole donor of satisfaction and punishment, may take on the stature and importance of a father figure—the one the source loves but hates and wants to castrate. Intense hatred and warm feelings often make faithful friends.

4. REGRESSION AS RORSCHACH:

When the binding ropes are released and
the source is dropped one foot,

then another foot, then again,
and so on and so on,

the rhythm of elevation, descent, known as "squassation",
reaches its climax when the source's torso

lands in the fetal pose.

5. MIND YOUR P's AND Q's:

Full-blown DDD (depression, debility, dread) syndrome
constitutes a state of discomfort that is well nigh intolerable.

The source sinks into defensive apathy from which it is hard
to arouse him.

Marshal your quick wit, good judgment and perfect timing
to prevent such collapse.

6. THE BEAUTY OF ISOLATION:

A cell that is soundproof, odorless, and totally dark can
produce results in a few hours or days, while detention in
an ordinary cell may produce results only after weeks or
months of confinement.

Speedy onset of anxiety is of great benefit to you in fulfilling
your mission.

Finally, bear in mind a water tank or iron lung is more effective than a cell.

7. DURESS, COMPLIANCE, REGRESSION
   ARE THE HOLY TRINITY OF COERCIVE
   INTERROGATION:

   You are in the service of your country.

   You are helping to make the world a better place.

ushered in with cleavage and a waltz

the fright of light
whites

dead eyes behind masks

and unseeing claimed/shamed

by the slow peepshow of desire

―――――

lies lie in wait in the conjugal streets

(notseeing of eyes wide)

(ghosttown of closed lids)

―――――

cowled poseurs
flower in from the night

lean lithe long-legged flaneurs

(without their understories)

―――――

the carnal carapace stalks its uncertainties
rainbows crest and foreshadowings foreplay

A storm careens from the east
  and acid rains make vegetation cower.

Asphodel, rose, columbine
Lie down among dandelions…

Clouds crouch while deserts flash
And roads are gashed by thrusts of broken glass.

The ontogeny is tired.

In desperate rendezvous our plenitude cries stop.

No eye cocked toward heaven, no remedy in unchecked want—

An insistent voice peals
Through the bruising wind:

   "My name is Ozymandias, king of kings:
   Look on my works, ye Mighty, and despair."

What audacity with no time (desire?) to atone for our lives?

ACT IV

Logos Besieged

A HISTORY OF TIME III

Our house burns in the snow

    At the edge of blond light

        Walls are drifts of snow

> *She is like the merchants' ships,*
> *She bringeth her food from afar.*
> *She girdeth her loins with strength,*
> *And strengtheneth her arms.*

We do not fear the snow
Plunging in tattered bolts to the ground

             The seams of our robes
             Are frayed by time

      The scarlet sun ignites each face

We recall the future
Reserve the past
Write memories on an unruled page

Syllables seek haven in our eyes

> *…everything that reminds me of her*
> *goes through me like a spear*

Arms on the white sheet
Head on the white case

      And the real terror of eternity
      In the black earth

The never coming back heads home

*The Gramineous Bicycle Garnished with Bells
and the Echinoderms
Bending the Spine to Look for Caresses*

*Behold, the people shall rise up as a great lion,
and lift up himself as a young lion: he shall not
lie down until he eat of the prey,
and drink the blood of the slain*

*The time for the unreal on the stage had arrived.
It was necessary to picture not life itself as it takes place in reality,
but as we vaguely feel it in our dreams,
our visions, our moments of spiritual uplift,*

OUR DESPAIR

Murmur to the silent earth

We're pedaling

DEUS EX MACHINA SPEAKS

Give me the altitude from which to peer down,
the deepest wound from which to look out,
a tiny candle to light the regions which will not ignite,
a shovel to dig shadows, a broom to sweep shadows away,
a thick stick to startle the dozing facts

A HISTORY OF TIME IV

welcome to oblivion

identity dissolves on this fool's page,

in memory of the past

black and white and the vast terrain
of gray between

all lies suppressed

forever hidden,
the world's riddle
only consciousness made real

the word fails, the heart fails,
light forsakes the sky

all things confess their ashes

ADDENDUM TO NOTES:
COERCIVE COUNTERINTELLIGENCE
INTERROGATION OF RESISTANT SOURCES

Welcome to today's class on techniques of post-collapse diagnosis
in the praxis of "Coercive Interrogation"——*(just in case)*

Ask your source to smile.

Ask your source to speak—

a simple sentence will do—

but coherently—

It is sunny today

I peed, then brushed my teeth

Ask your source to raise both arms—

Ask your source to stick out his tongue.

(NOTA BENE: *If the tongue is 'crooked', if it goes to one side
or the other it is an indication of a stroke.*)

If your source has trouble with ANY ONE of these tasks, call an
emergency squad immediately!!

AND describe the symptoms to the dispatcher.

A cardiologist says if everyone in CI
        learns this technique
and shares it with 10 people

You can bet at least one life will be saved.

HEINRICH HEINE SPEAKS

At first I almost despaired,
And I thought I could never bear it;
And yet I have borne it—
Only do not ask me how.

I beg you

Quantify me

        I am proof of the disproof

           of the unproof

Matter

    Forced by the
        gravity of
            the situation

To spin
Where you can
Not find me

        Through zeroes

            ghost on the tail of the
              void-bent
                  black-holed
                     slug-borne

green things nowhere

PRESENT TENSE VI

The Power to Die's an Empty Gun

Going on embraces weeds.

Life and the outside world will never be better.

I have always been a realist.

What is the next move, world
The next renovation?
Must we keep taking turns dying on you?

I don't forget;
I mark the names once more:
you shtetl Brok,
you pines,
you Jews
who climbed on board,
whose veins raced faster
than the train

We wanted to give all we had, to revel in the known,
To achieve our common goal

Barbarians have slipped through
The interstices of the hierarchy

Violence took root long ago in the natural history of enchantment

It's too late to cry

A sparrow strays, unruffled here among
crumpled leaves, on starling turf, alone,
to nab her share of seed and crumb strewn
in the street. Outnumbered, dwarfed, talons
planted at the verge where battle lurks.

                         A flock of starlings,
Glowing black plumage pied by errant
Light; splayed feet arranged and rearranged
On cobblestone; incessant banter of wings;
Canter of webbed feet, groans, complaints
From beaks, scumbled gutteral thirst, chirps.

          Come, tiny thing, *spizella*,
                    Stake your claim.

MARINE EXPERT SPEAKS

No one anticipated the potential magnitude
Of the jellyfish invasion—

From Barcelona to Sydney,
New York to Tokyo
Faceless marauders roamed the global warming.

More jellyfish in more seas
Children at play in the waves

Tentacles arouse as they brush young loins
More venom lusts in the deep—

The sea is sick.

Beaches must close.
Blue flags rise.

Something is trying to reach us. It is saying,
"Look how badly you are treating me."

A HISTORY OF TIME V

We sit chilled
Arms wrapped
In the posture
Of gathering heat
Plagued wills
Swaddled in the furnace

Of winter and decline

        Season of decline
        Skins whiten
        Waters ice

Ice-sparked stars
Banished to a blood-
Stained sky
Tortures torment
The documentary screen

Stop, stop, start

But we prevail

        As we prevail
        Frigid air
        Gropes inland

Inland where soil
Warms for longer
Growing seasons—

Potatoes in Ireland
Grass in the low
Countries,
       in Hokkaido
           commas of rice

In young sun

Roosters claw at hard soil
Squads of locusts lurch like hail
Mums preen between jagged rocks

Snakes, butterflies, caterpillars
Squirm, spiders twist, frogs hunker beneath the lotus leaf

A skull and shattered ribcage bleach at the edge of the lake

Detail is reason

        Presence absence

Life unknowable

Ito Jakuchi knows what he sees when he sees it, that good looker

EPILOGUE

Mulch Beneath Juniper

ECOSYSTEM

1.

That somber greens—ferns, conifers, cycads—flittered
    with fruit and bloom

That the earth's face pinked, reddened, honeycombed glow

That angiosperm came to outnumber gymnosperm

That they seduced insect, bat and bird, flaunting colors
    and smelling good

That they multiplied, hybridized, colonized east to far,
    north to near, valley to peak

2.

That brush crowded out burr oak and big bluestem grass

That weed evicted sweet brown-eyed Susan

That buckthorn unseated cream gentian and violet bush clover

3.

That there had been prairie-fringed orchid, Indian grass,
    large-leafed aster

That there had grown starry campion and bottlebrush buckeye

That there had flown great spangled fritillaries, Edwards' Hairstreaks

That Cooper's hawks, eastern bluebirds, Appalachian browns
    had manned the trees

4.

That what was mis-taken reappeared

That flowers strummed in the trees

5.

That they made it and made it, new, now, and again

That it is possible, possible, spreading, and so

EXEUNT OMNES

NOTES, APPROPRIATIONS, SOURCES

"PRIMER":

Eternity..., Woody Allen.
The struggle..., Albert Camus, *The Myth of Sisyphus*.
It is not your obligation..., Rabbi Tarfon, *Pirke Avot* 2:16.
E cosi desiro..., Petrarch.
*All warfare...*Sun Tsu, *The Art of War*.
The soul..., Rumi
For we are but of yesterday..., Job 8:9

"CHIEF SEATTLE SPEAKS":

This is my lineation for Chief Seattle's response to the U.S. government during negotiations for the Treaty of Mukilteo, 1855.

"PRESENT TENSE II":

"Leash Girl" is the nickname bestowed upon Lynndie England after a photograph in which she was grinning as she held an Iraqi prisoner on a leash was leaked to the media in the Abu Ghraib prison abuse scandal.

"GUN MOOSE SNOW":

The female hunter I had in mind was Sarah Palin, a hunter in more ways than one.

"Where is the place that love dwelleth?":

"*Fear and sorrow........*", *The Anatomy of Melancholy* by Robert Burton.

"THE GOOD BOOK":

If I am not for myself....., Rabbi Hillel, *Pirke Avot 1:14*.
*Year after year...*a haiku by the Japanese poet, Basho.

"ANNA SPEAKS":
This poem appeared originally in my book, *At the Site of Inside Out*, published by the University of Massachusetts Press.

"ALBERT SIGMUND BITTER FRUIT":
This poem derives from a correspondence between Albert Einstein and Sigmund Freud published as *Why War?* shortly after Hitler came to power in 1933. The words addressed to Mankind in 1950 are those of Albert Einstein.

"WILLIAM SIEGFRIED BITTER ASPIC":
This poem is composed of lines from poems by William Blake and Siegfried Sassoon.

"I saw the survivors of a battle sending out postcards":
The opening quotation here is from "The Aleph" by Jorge Luis Borges.

"NOTES: COERCIVE COUNTERINTELLIGENCE INTERROGATION OF RESISTANT SOURCES":
This poem is indebted to two declassified CIA manuals, "Human Resource Exploitation Training Manual-1983" and "KUBARK Counterintelligence Interrogation-July 1963," released by the National Security Archive on May 12, 2004, delineating techniques still in use during the Bush administration.

"A HISTORY OF TIME III":
She is like..., Proverbs 31:14; 31:19
...everything that reminds me of her goes through me like a spear is from a letter John Keats wrote to Charles Armitage Brown, referring to Fanny Brawne.

"The never coming back heads home":

 The Gramineous Bicycle… comes from the title of Max Ernst's famous gouache of 1920-21. The complete title is "The gramineous bicycle garnished with bells the dappled fire damps and the echinoderms bending the spine to look for caresses."

 The time for the unreal on the stage………. was said by Stanislavsky as quoted by James Roose-Evans in *Experimental Theatre from Stanislavsky to Peter Brook.*

"HEINRICH HEINE SPEAKS":

 These words of Heinrich Heine—*Anfangs wollt' ich fast verzagen, und ich glaubt', ich trug es nie; Und ich hab' es doch getragen, Aber fragt mich nur nicht, wie?*—were gathered together in his *Lieder Buch,* and were set to music by many composers, most notably Robert Schumann. George Eliot, a great admirer of Heine's powers with language, wrote: "He indicates a whole sad history in a single quatrain: there is not an image in it, not a thought; but it is beautiful, simple and perfect as a 'big round tear'—it is pure feeling breathed in pure music."

ACKNOWLEDGMENTS

With gratitude to life, planet earth, culture, humanity, reason, and their discontents.

"Anna Speaks" (formerly "Confession") originally appeared in *At the Site of Inside Out*, University of Massachusetts Press.

Gratitude, too, to the editors of the following publications where these "happenings" first appeared in one form or another:

American Letters & Commentary: "Primer," "Present Tense I," "Present Tense II," "Present Tense III."

Alaska Quarterly Review: "A war by any other name would smell as" (formerly "A Rose By Any Other Name Might Smell As").

Barrow Street: "Ecosystem," "A History of Time V" (formerly "A History of Time III").

Chimera Review: "Oh gods have you forsaken us…" (formerly "American Beauty").

Denver Quarterly: "Present Tense V," "Deus Ex Machina Speaks."

Istanbul Literary Review: "A History of Time III," "Belated kerfuffle…" (formerly "Wages of Sin"), "The new century…." (formerly "Ur Spectacle"), "The one who hardens the heart" (formerly "Inaudible Prayer"), "ushered in with cleavage…" (formerly "Home Fires Burn"), "Taped from Earlier Live Podcasts."

Runes: "In this time" (formerly "Currency").

Verse: "Millennia are held at bay,…" (formerly "Windows").

"All afternoon alterities…" appeared as "Bricolage: Versicolor." in *Poetry After 9/11: An Anthology of New York Poets*, Dennis Loy Johnson and Valerie Merians, eds.

Anna Rabinowitz has published three books of poetry, *The Wanton Sublime: A Florilegium of Whethers and Wonders*, Tupelo, 2006, *Darkling*, Tupelo, 2001 (which will be translated into German and published by Luxbooks, Wiesbaden, Germany, forthcoming 2010), and *At the Site of Inside Out*, University of Massachusetts Press 1997. *Darkling* was a finalist for *ForeWord Magazine*'s Best Poetry Book of 2001 Award and was nominated for a Pushcart Prize in 2002, and *At the Site of Inside Out* was a winner of the Juniper Prize. American Opera Projects transformed *Darkling* into an experimental opera-theatre work that blurs distinctions between poetry, theater, and music. This production had its world premiere to great critical acclaim on February 26, 2006 at the 13th Street Theatre, New York City. A National Endowment for the Arts Fellow for 2001, Anna Rabinowitz has published widely in such journals as *Atlantic Monthly, Boston Review, The Paris Review, Colorado Review, Southwest Review, Denver Quarterly, Sulfur, LIT, VOLT, Verse,* and *Doubletake*. Her work has also been reprinted in *The Best American Poetry* 1989, edited by Donald Hall, *Life on the Line: Selections on Words and Healing, The KGB Bar Reader, The Poets' Grimm, Poetry Daily,* and *Poetry After 9/11.*